USS LOUISVILLE CA-28

WARSHIP PICTORIAL #3

CLASSIC WARSHIPS PUBLISHING

Editor - Steve Wiper
Layout - T.A.Flowers
Illustrations - T.A.Flowers

Current titles in print from
CLASSIC WARSHIPS PUBLISHING

USS INDIANAPOLIS CA-35

USS MINNEAPOLIS CA-36

Look for these exciting subjects in future books from

CLASSIC WARSHIPS PUBLISHING

Yorktown Class Carrier

Alaska Class Cruiser

Des Moines Class Cruiser

Benson Class Destroyer

Myoko Class Cruiser

Copyright © 1998

**CLASSIC WARSHIPS
PUBLISHING**

P.O.Box 57591 • Tucson AZ 85732
ISBN #0-9654829-2-8

November 11, 1942: Mare Island, California - The USS Louisville leaves port bound for Pearl Harbor, Hawaii. After escorting troop transports as far as New Caledonia, she will join up with Task Force 67 at Espiritu Santos.

April 7, 1945: Mare Island, California - Almost identical photo of the Louisville in her late wartime configuration. The vessel has just completed major repairs, necessary from damage caused by two Japanese kamikaze strikes.

USS Louisville CA 28
Northampton Class Cruiser
Operational history

1924

US Congress authorized Pensacola and Northampton Class Cruisers. President Coolidge delayed construction of Northampton Class ships until 1927.

1928

<u>July 4</u> - Keel laid down at Puget Sound Navy Yard in Bremerton, Washington.

1930

<u>September 1</u> - Launched; sponsored by Miss Jane Brown Kennedy.

1931

<u>January 15</u> - Commissioned, with Capt. E.J. Marquart as ship's first captain.
<u>July 1</u> - Officially designated as hull number CA-28.
<u>Summer</u> - Began shakedown cruise from Bremerton to New York City via the Panama Canal.

1932

Returned from New York to participate in 1932 fleet problems. Later committed to gunnery exercises in San Pedro-San Diego area.

1933

<u>Winter</u> - Sailed for Hawaii and participated in naval exercises there. Returned to the west coast (San Pedro, California) to become a school-ship for anti-aircraft training.

1934

<u>April</u> - Departed San Diego to begin nine month voyage "showing the flag" at various ports in Central America, the Caribbean and along the US gulf and eastern coasts.
<u>December</u> - Returned to the California coast and participated in gunnery and tactical exercises into the following year.

1935

<u>Spring</u> - Departed for Dutch Harbor, Alaska. Later in the year, arrived at Pearl Harbor, Hawaii to take part in fleet problems.

1936

<u>Spring</u> - Active in Fleet Problem 18 off Panama.
<u>November</u> - Sailed with other members of the fleet and President Franklin D. Roosevelt on the "Good Neighbor" tour of South America, including the Pan American Conference in Buenos Aires.

1937

Carried out further exercises in the Pacific Ocean.

1938

<u>January</u> - Began long Pacific cruise to Hawaii, Samoa, Tahiti and Australia. While in Sydney, rescued passengers from a ferryboat which had capsized. The small ship rolled over when the passengers all rushed to one side to see the passing Louisville. Returned to Pearl Harbor later in the fall.

1939

<u>Winter</u> - Took part in fleet exercises in the Caribbean.
<u>May</u> - Returned to the west coast. Participated in fleet problems off Hawaii.
<u>August</u> - Departed Long Beach, California, for Bahia, Brazil via the Panama Canal. Received orders there to proceed to Simonstown, South Africa. Because of the war in Europe (U-Boat threat), the American flag was spot-lighted on the voyage across the Atlantic. Returned to New York with 148 million dollars in British gold for safe deposit in the United States.

1941

<u>December 7</u> - Escorted troopships from Tarakan, East Borneo, to Pearl Harbor. Proceeded on to San Diego, California.

1942

<u>January 6</u> - Sailed as part of Task Force 17 bound for Samoa.
<u>January 22</u> - Landed troops on Samoa Island. Returned to Pearl Harbor after taking part in raids by carrier planes against the Gilbert and Marshall Islands. During this action, one seaplane was lost.
<u>February</u> - Patrolled the Canton-Ellice area to protect US bases there.
<u>March/April</u> - Joined Task Force 11 in operations against enemy positions in the Bismarck Archipelago and Solomon Island chain.

May - Returned to West Coast for refitting and additional armament.

June-September - Joined Task Force 8 in the Aleutians to provide convoy escort. Shelled the island of Kiska.

September-November - Back at Mare Island.

November 11 - Departed Mare Island for return to duty in the South Pacific, escorting troop ships as far as New Caledonia. Later Joined Task Force 67 at Esprito Santo to assist in the Solomons campaign.

1943

January 29 - In company with TF 18, took part in the *Battle of Rennel Island.* Hit by one dud torpedo. Took the wounded heavy cruiser Chicago under tow for ten hours only to loose her during the next enemy air raid.

April - Sailed for the the Aleutians via Pearl Harbor to join Task force 16.

May 11-30 - Supported the assault and occupation of Attu, Alaska.

July - Participated in the bombardment of Kiska Island.

August-September - Provided convoy escort in northern Pacific waters.

October-December - Returned to Mare Island for major overhaul, weapon and radar additions.

1944

January - Returned to South Pacific as flagship of Rear Adm. Oldendorf.

January 29 - Began extensive shelling campaign with the island of Wotje in the Marshalls.

February - Participated in the bombardment against Roi and Namur islands until their capture on the 3rd.

February 17-22 - Led gunfire support group against Eniwetok Island.

March - Joined fast carrier Task Force 58. Participated in the pre-invasion bombardment against the Palaus Islands.

April - Assisted in the bombardment of the islands of Truk and Sawatan.

June - Provided 11 continuous days of fire support against Siapan.

July-August - Conducted shelling operations against Japanese defenders on Tinian and Guam.

September - Receives approximately two weeks leave before returning to duty with pre-invasion support against Peleliu Island.

October 17 - Enters Leyte Gulf in support of major allied invasion force and shells shore installations for seven straight days.

October 24-25 - In company with seven more heavy cruisers and six battleships, engaged a Japanese support fleet at *The Battle of Surigo Strait.* The result was a major loss for the Japanese and denied them of any hope of supporting their ground positions on Leyte.

November-December -Rejoined the fast carriers of now designated TF 38 and participated in the pre-invasion strikes against the Japanese on Luzon.

1945

January 5 - While en route to support Allied landings at Lingayen Gulf, crashed by two Japanese kamikaze aircraft causing extensive damage. 32 seamen killed, 56 wounded. Completed shelling assignment and downed several enemy aircraft.

January 6 - Withdrew from combat area and proceeded to Mare Island for repairs.

February-April - Under repair for major damage caused during Philippines campaign .

May - Returned to the Pacific theater to join TF 54 to provide fire cover for Allied ground forces on Okinawa.

June 5 - Crashed a second time by a single kamikaze, causing minor damage and killing only one sailor.

June 9 - After temporary repairs by the crew, continued her fire cover duties.

June 15 - Ordered to retire and proceed to Pearl Harbor for repairs.

August-September - Supervised evacuation of Allied POWs at Darien, Manchuria. Escorted surrendered Japanese vessels from Tsingato, China to Jinsen, Korea. Returned to Chefoo, China.

October - Joined Allied Force operating in Yellow Sea, supervising the return of Japanese troops to Japan from China and Korea.

1946

Early - Sailed for the East coast via San Pedro, California.

June 17 - Decommissioned and placed in reserve in the Atlantic Reserve Fleet at the Philadelphia Navy Yard.

1947-1958

In storage. Was occasionally stripped of fittings, weapons, etc. and repainted every few years, but otherwise unused along with the rest of the "Mothball Fleet".

1959

March 1 - Stricken from the US Navy roster.

September 14 - Sold to the Marlene Blouse Corporation of New York and soon scrapted for her metal.

Awarded a total of 13 Battle Stars for service in World War Two.

June 3, 1930: Puget Sound Navy Yard, Bremerton, Washington - Various structures emerge from the deck as the Louisville nears completion. The main mast rises in the foreground, straddling the aft fire control position. Further forward, up the wide stairs, four newly installed 5 in. anti-aircraft guns sit under protective canvas on the lower gun deck. The upper gun deck over the hangar is awaiting the #2 funnel and the large aircraft crane. A huge tent of canvas covers the entire center of the ship as machinery and boiler spaces are finished underneath. The forward tripod mast (right) can really be appreciated here, as it soars better than 120ft. above the ship's keel.

August 27, 1930: Puget Sound, Washington - Only four more days until launching. The ship is still missing the aircraft catapults and on the deck above the hangar, the aircraft crane waits for installation in front of the #2 funnel. Her 21 in. torpedo tubes are visible just aft of the gangplank.

When coal-fired ships evolved into oil-fired ships, petroleum in the form of fuel and lubricants found its way into the harbor waters. The wide black "Boot Topping" at the water line came into existence as a means to hide the unsightly oil ring around the ship.

February 2, 1931: Puget Sound, Washington, Dry Dock #2 - The Louisville was built with ranging clocks on the fore and main masts. Developed in the early 1900s as a means of firing coordination, these dials became obsolete as battle distances increased. Her range clocks and torpedo tube compliment will be landed at a later date. New thinking believed the torpedoes to be too hazardous. A new armored rangefinder sits above the navigation bridge.

April 22, 1935: San Pedro, California - On the #2 funnel a large "E" bears tribute to excellence in recent gunnery practice. The long opening in her side is where the original torpedo tubes were located. Off the starboard bow is a New Orleans Class cruiser, the USS Tuscaloosa or San Francisco.

July 17, 1938: Ketchikan, Alaska - Nearly ten years old and appearing very much the same as when she was built. The paint scheme is Standard Navy Gray (a). Search lights mounted on the foremast are 24 in.; the four on the mainmast are 36 in. An angled cap has been added to the #1 funnel to divert smoke away from the bridge area.

January 1, 1942: Mare Island - Still in a pre-war paint scheme, the Louisville sports the unusual Measure 1 camouflage. Dark Gray (5-D) from waterline to somewhere above the funnel tops. The second color is Light Gray (5-L). She has mounted four 3 in. guns for additional anti-aircraft defense.

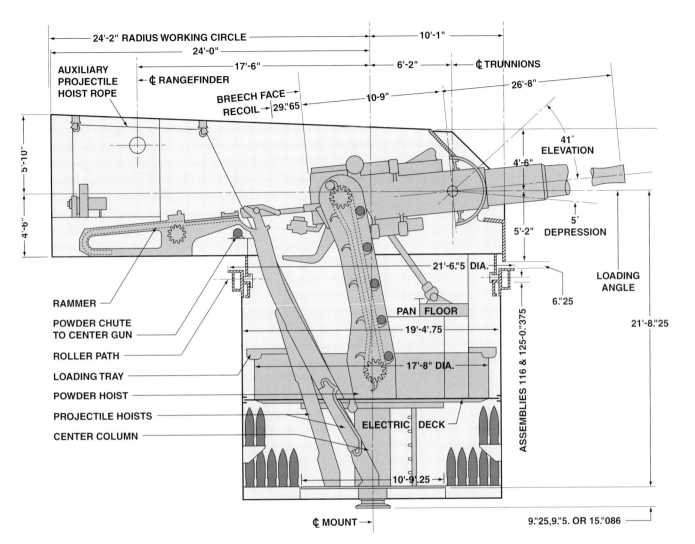

24'-2" RADIUS WORKING CIRCLE
24'-0"
17'-6"
10'-1"
6'-2"
¢ TRUNNIONS

AUXILIARY PROJECTILE HOIST ROPE
¢ RANGEFINDER
26'-8"
BREECH FACE
RECOIL 29."65
10-9"

5'-10"
4'-6"

41° ELEVATION
4'-6"
5° DEPRESSION
5'-2"

RAMMER
POWDER CHUTE TO CENTER GUN
ROLLER PATH
LOADING TRAY
POWDER HOIST
PROJECTILE HOISTS
CENTER COLUMN

21'-6."5 DIA.
LOADING ANGLE
6."25

PAN FLOOR
19'-4'.75
17'-8" DIA.

ASSEMBLIES 116 & 125-0.'375
21'-8."25

ELECTRIC DECK

10'-9'.25
¢ MOUNT
9."25,9."5. OR 15."086

8 in/55 calibre gun

Mk 14

Bore	8 in.
Weight	30.0 tons
Length oa.	449 in.
Length bore	437.6 in.
Length chamber	60.0 in.
Volume chamber	4860 in.^{3}
Length rifling	373.65 in.
Weight projectile	260 lb.
Propellant charge	90 lb. NC
Muzzle velocity	2800 f/s
Working pressure	17 tons/in.^{2}
Approx life	715 EFC
Max range	31860 yd.
Rate of Fire	2.1 spm.

The 8in. guns of the USS Louisville were of the 14/0 series.

illustration redrawn from USN documents

The 8 in. gun was in use in the 1880s and very popular with the US and Japanese Navies before the Second World War. The US used the gun as the secondary armament on pre-Dreadnought battleships often in a unique double-storied turret. The Japanese used it only in their armored cruisers. Primarily due to its long range, the US selected the 8 in gun in 1919-1930 for use in a series of Pacific cruisers. From this the 8 in. limit on cruiser armament was established under the terms of the Washington Treaty of 1922. The 8 in. or foreign 203 mm gun became the primary armament for large cruisers for all navies and was mounted mostly in twin and triple mounts. In the US navy the gun was found in triple turrets on the Pensacola, Northampton, New Orleans, Portland and Baltimore class cruisers. It was paired up in twin turrets on the Pensacola and Salt lake City as well as the aircraft carriers Lexington and Saratoga. The different Mks. or models varied mostly by small differences and all were essentially the same weapon. The last large triple turrets were composed of Mk. 16s, mounted on the Des Moines Class cruisers. These guns fired 'fixed ammunition' at the incredible rate of one shell every 6 seconds.

12 *May 26, 1942: Mare Island - The Louisville in the last stages of her first wartime refit. New 20 mm guns are positioned on the bow, on the command level, and on the forward lookout platform. A Mk19 director sits far forward on the chart house deck, replacing a 12 ft. armored rangefinder which has been moved up to the lookout level. Next to Louisville, the light cruiser USS Helena will soon join the war after repair of torpedo damage suffered in the Japanese attack on Pearl Harbor.*

13 *Wind deflectors cover a good portion of the flag and signal bridge wings as well as the shield around the Mk19 director. All three are of different configuration. A new quad 1.1 in. anti-aircraft gun has replaced an old 3 in./50 single under the flag deck overhang. It's director, a Mk44 unit, sits in a little tub above on the navigation wing.*

14 *Splinter shielding has been erected around the open mounted 5 in. guns. Another 1.1 in. quad has replaced the mid ship 3 in/50 gun. The aft Mk19 director, which once sat in the open area behind the #2 funnel, now is perched high on the tripod mainmast surrounded by four new 20 mm guns.*

13

798-42　　　　　U.S.S. LOUISVILLE.

LAN VIEW AFT.

ARE ISLAND, CAL.　　　MAY 26, 1942

May 26, 1942: Mare Island - Beautiful photo of Louisville's stern shows the heavy hemp mooring lines. Leaning off the stern are eight smoke generators and another pair of new 20mm anti-aircraft guns. Above the recently moved Mk19 director, a Mk4 radar screen has been installed. The ship's name on the stern is 1/4 in. steel plates, cut out and welded to the hull. Steel disks have also been welded over the lower scuttle openings to increase watertightness.

May 26, 1942 - USS Louisville departing port soon, to team up with Task Force 16 for the assault on the Japanese-occupied Aleutian Islands off Alaska. For air defense she now carries four quad 1.1 in guns and 12 single 20 mm guns. All 50 cal. machine guns (now obsolete) have been removed. The armor belt is clearly visible amidships. The strange apparatus at the waterline just below the #3 turret is the prop guard. This structure prevented damage to the propellers should the ship contact an object such as a pier or another ship.

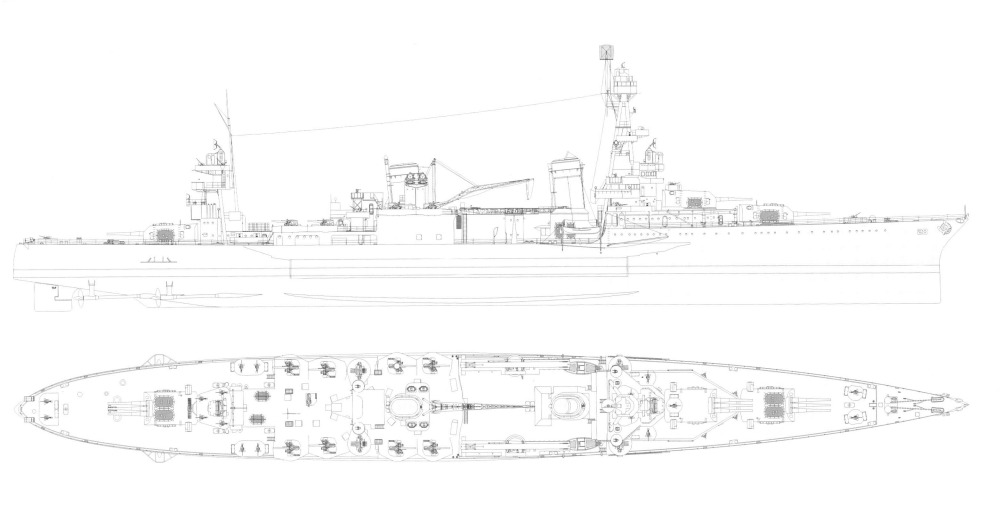

USS Louisville
November, 1942

scale 1/700

6946-42
PLAN VIEW, FORWARD

November 10, 1942 - USS Louisville back at Mare Island for overhaul and weapon systems upgrade. Circled in white: a new 20mm gun positioned atop #2 turret, a platform added to the front of the navigation level and a pair of handling davits just behind the focsle level on the main deck. The small circular disks on the mooring lines are to keep rats from climbing on or off the ship.

19

Close-up view of the back of the forward superstructure and the #1 funnel. On the main deck, in the white circles, the new davits and 26 ft. motor whaleboats are now stored abreast the #1 funnel. All other small launches have been removed to make room for additional anti-aircraft weapons. In the background, three destroyers receive service: (nearest) an unidentified Benham class ship, a Benson and a Porter.

18

6917-42   (CA-38)
PLAN VIEW, AMIDSHIPS.
MARE ISLAND, CAL.   NOVEMBER 16, 1942

19

November 10, 1942 - A nice close-up view of the quad 1.1 in. mount sitting on the extension off the command platform. The quad 1.1 in. weapon was of 75 cal, recoil operated and water cooled. Each barrel was fed by eight-round clips. The four-barreled mount could fire up to 150 rounds per minute. Maximum range was 7400 yds. with a ceiling of 19,000 ft. The 1.1 in. was complicated and proved unreliable in service and would soon be replaced. The Mk 44 director on the navigation wing above has been replaced with a new model, the Mk 51.

21

Looking under the mainmast, the large white circle shows the vacancy left after the removal of the boat crane. The removal of the ship's boats on the lower gun deck has allowed for the addition of two stacks of life rafts. In a sinking condition, the life rafts would be much quicker and easier to launch than boats. Down on the main deck, two large tubs with a pair of 20 mm guns are fitted where the captain's launch was once stored. A small shield has been fitted between the new Mk 51 directors abaft the funnel. The position was probably an auxiliary conning station.

November 11, 1942 - Louisville departs Mare Island bound for Pearl Harbor. Her camouflage has been the same since April (Sea Blue 5-S). This particular camouflage sacrificed surface concealment (dark silhouette) with the ability to blend in with the ocean when viewed from above (enemy aircraft). Notice the center barrel on the #3 turret is in a recoil position probably for maintenance.

November 29, 1942 - It would appear that during her stop at Pearl Harbor (prior to the rendezvous with troop transports headed for New Caledonia) an additional 20mm gun was added to the top of #3 turret. On the foremast, another 20mm position has been created after the removal of the 12ft. armored rangefinder.

December 17, 1943: Mare Island, California - A leaner, meaner Louisville emerges from her first major refit in over a year. Immediately noticeable is the topping of the foremast and the new fire control platform. The navigation and signal platforms are now much narrower. Her anti-aircraft defenses are bolstered by the addition of the new hard-hitting 40mm Bofors, in twin and quad mountings. Measure 32–6D camouflage replaces the old paint scheme.

25

A new 20mm position has been created just aft of the #1 turret. In addition, all of the 20mm guns have been refitted to lighter bases and now use an electronic gun sight. Smaller life rafts replace larger ones on the side of #1 turret and on top, stacks of floater netshave been added.

26

The forward superstructure has been radically modified to reduce top hamper and to lower the center of gravity. A single mast extension has been added to the foremast to accommodate the new huge SK air search antenna and the small surface search unit, SG. Under the dark canvas cover is the Mk8 antenna mounted above the Mk34 main director. Two white circles toward the bottom of the photo show one of the new quad 40mm guns and another new 20mm gun crammed into the passageway abreast the command platform.

27

Another pair of 20mm guns have been mounted abreast the funnel and a small structure erected just aft. A close examination shows the new camouflage scheme is unfinished (back of #1 funnel, port catapult tower). In the lower right, legs of the new mainmast straddle the #2 funnel. One of the 36in. searchlights has been landed and a small flag locker takes its place.

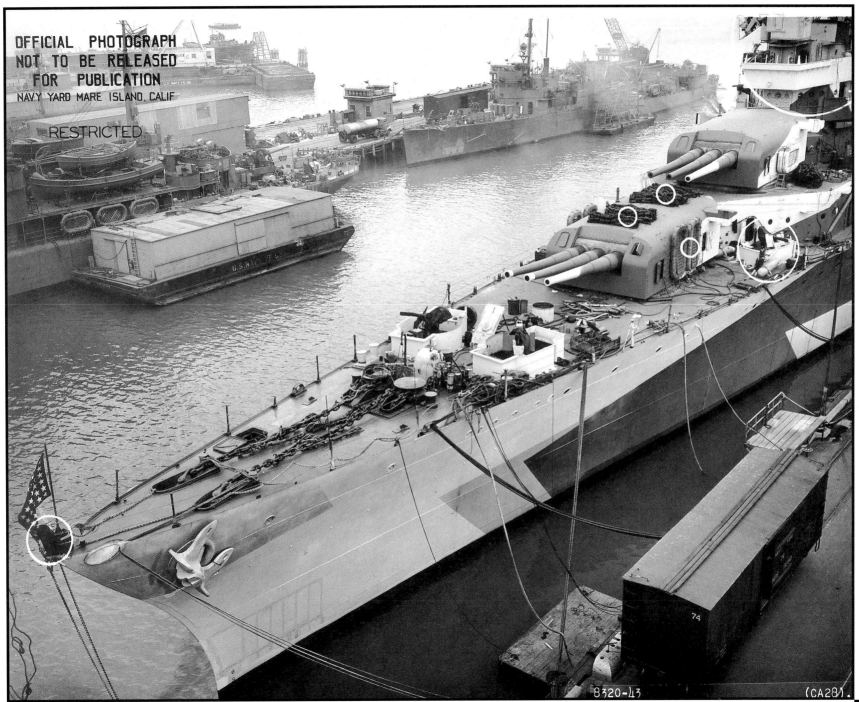

8320-43

(CA28).

8319-43   (CA28).
PLAN VIEW, AMIDSHIPS LOOKING AFT.
MARE ISLAND, CAL.   17 DECEMBER 1943.

8323-45   (CA28).
PLAN VIEW, AMIDSHIPS LOOKING FORWARD.
MARE ISLAND, CAL   17 DECEMBER 1943

USS LOUISVILLE
DECEMBER 1943

scale 1/350

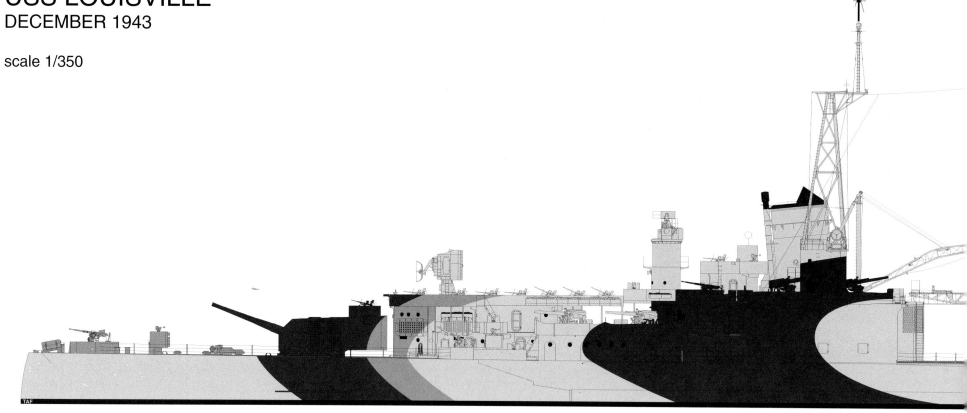

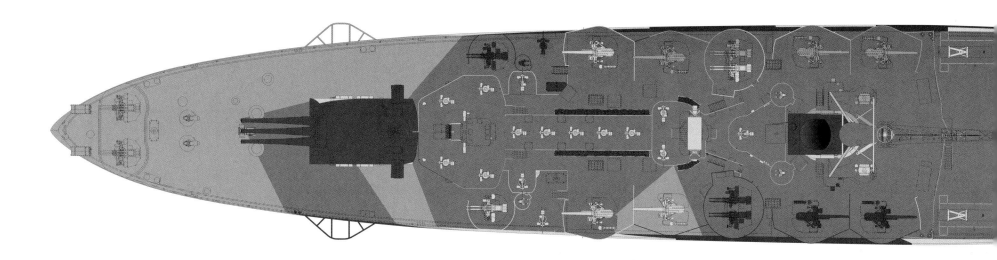

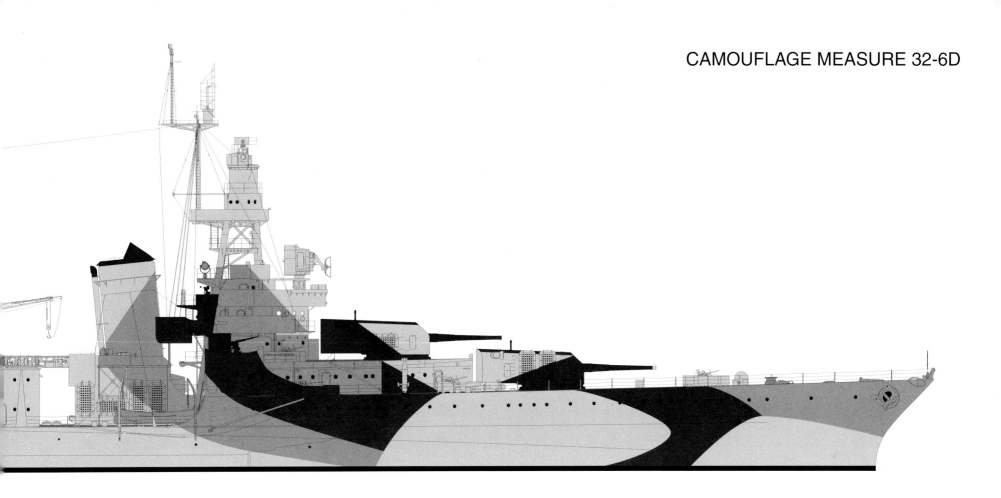

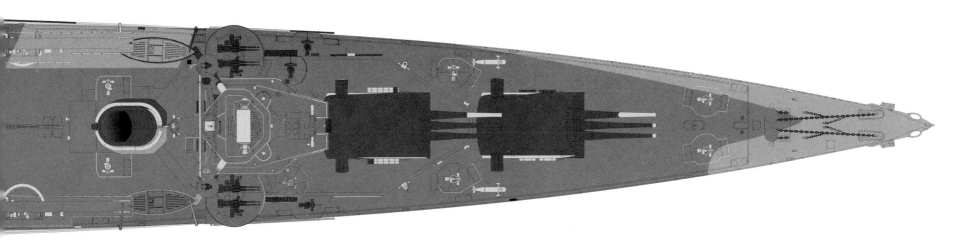

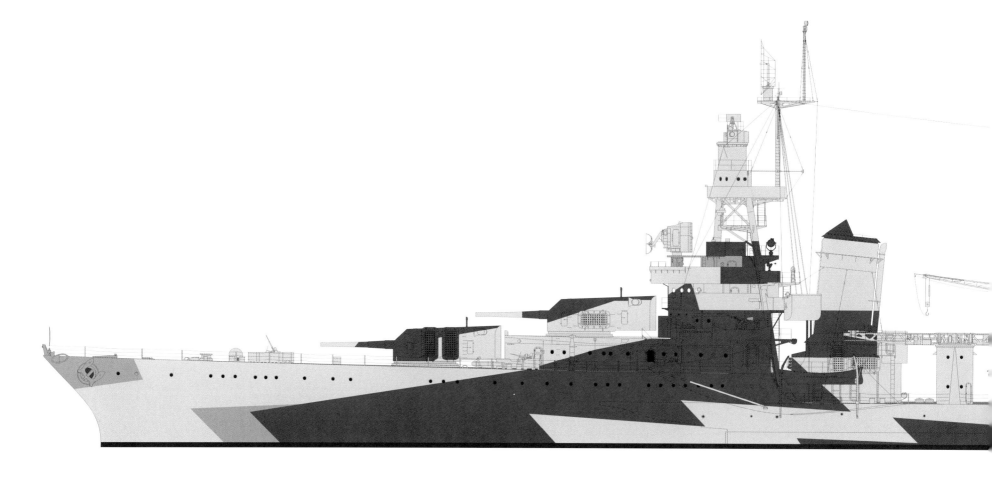

From December, 1943, to April, 1945, the USS Louisville was camouflaged in what was offi-
cially known as Measure 32-6D. As with all camouflage schemes, the underlying objective
is to use the pattern which is most effective in the period of greatest danger. While the 32-
6D design appears to make the ship more visible, the bold contrast and irregular shapes
tend to hamper identification, course and range. It was found to be the best overall camouflage against enemy submarines in areas of high visibility and also the best scheme when it
cannot be predetermined where vessels will operate or what light and weather conditions
will be encountered. This measure was designed differently for each side of the ship to
maintain the camouflage's effect and avoid symmetry when viewed end-on.

32	6	D
COLOR(S)	PATTERN	VARIANT

The US Navy (more than any other navy) took the theory of ship camouflage and developed it into a science. Hundreds of measures were experimented with and scores of different measures were adopted at one time or another.

 Light Gray (5-L)

 Ocean Gray (5-0)

 Deck Blue (20-B)

 Dull Black (BK)

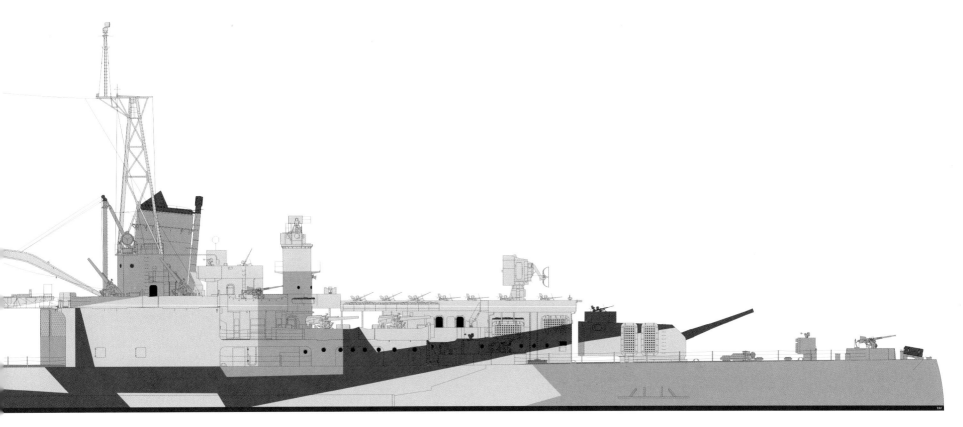

December 17, 1943

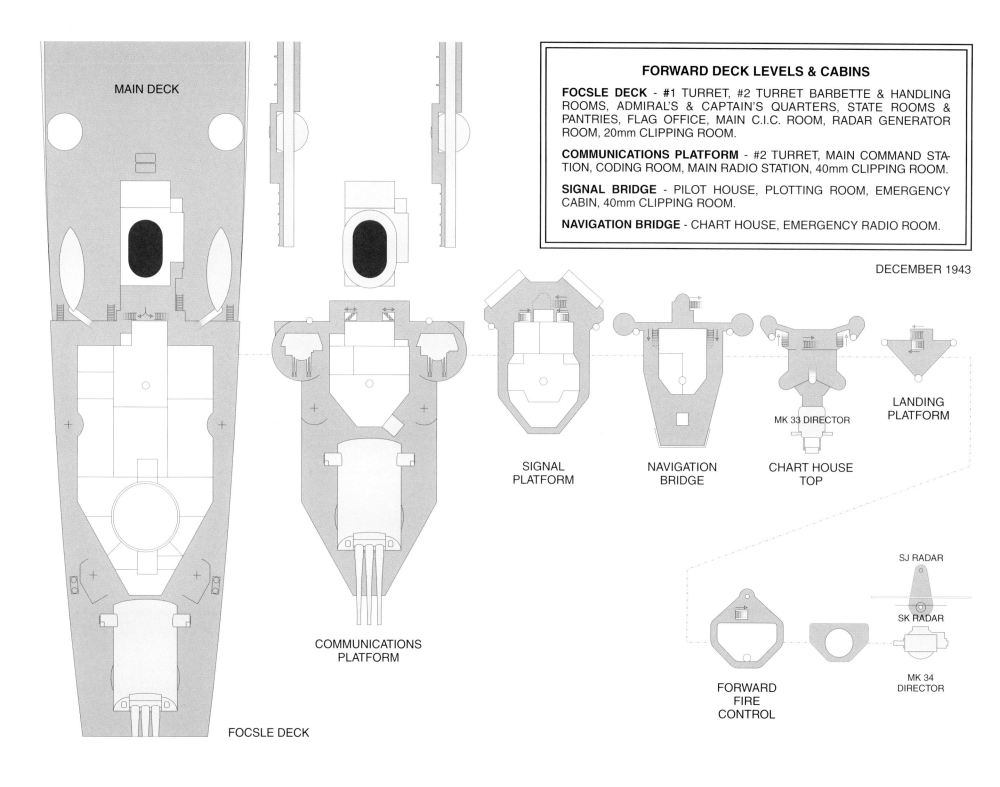

MAIN DECK

FORWARD DECK LEVELS & CABINS

FOCSLE DECK - #1 TURRET, #2 TURRET BARBETTE & HANDLING ROOMS, ADMIRAL'S & CAPTAIN'S QUARTERS, STATE ROOMS & PANTRIES, FLAG OFFICE, MAIN C.I.C. ROOM, RADAR GENERATOR ROOM, 20mm CLIPPING ROOM.

COMMUNICATIONS PLATFORM - #2 TURRET, MAIN COMMAND STATION, CODING ROOM, MAIN RADIO STATION, 40mm CLIPPING ROOM.

SIGNAL BRIDGE - PILOT HOUSE, PLOTTING ROOM, EMERGENCY CABIN, 40mm CLIPPING ROOM.

NAVIGATION BRIDGE - CHART HOUSE, EMERGENCY RADIO ROOM.

DECEMBER 1943

SIGNAL
PLATFORM

NAVIGATION
BRIDGE

CHART HOUSE
TOP

MK 33 DIRECTOR

LANDING
PLATFORM

COMMUNICATIONS
PLATFORM

FOCSLE DECK

FORWARD
FIRE
CONTROL

MK 34
DIRECTOR

SJ RADAR

SK RADAR

MIDSHIP & AFT
DECK LEVELS & CABINS

MAIN DECK - #3 TURRET, OFFICER'S & CREW'S GALLEY, VEGETABLE LOCKER, BUTCHER SHOP, BAKERY, SHIPFITTER & CARPENTER SHOP, PHOTO LAB, BOAT MOTOR SHOP, AA REPAIR SHOP, CREW'S WASHROOM & W.C.

LOWER GUN DECK - 5in GUN STATIONS, AUX. C.I.C. ROOM, CATAPULT TOWERS, AIRCRAFT HANGAR SPACES, AVIATION WORKSHOP & STOREROOM, RADAR TRANSMISSION ROOM, ORDNANCE WORKSHOP, OPTICAL SHOP, 40mm CLIPPING ROOMS.

UPPER GUN DECK - 5in GUN STATIONS, AFT FIRE CONTROL STATION, RADIO TRANSMISSION ROOM, SECONDARY STEERING, 20mm AIRCRAFT DEFENSE.

SCALE 1/350

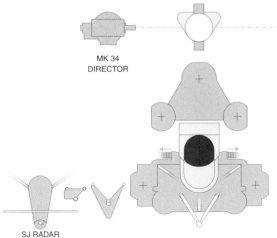

MK 34
DIRECTOR

SJ RADAR

RADAR
PLATFORM

SEARCHLIGHT
PLATFORM

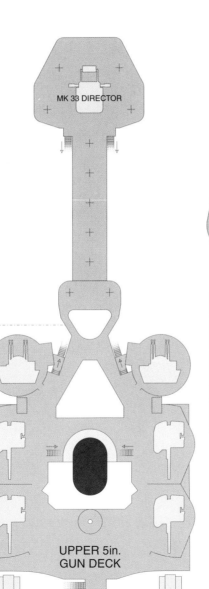

MK 33 DIRECTOR

UPPER 5in.
GUN DECK

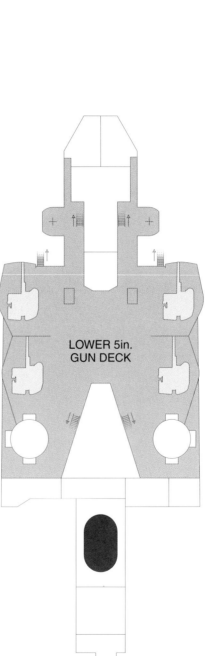

LOWER 5in.
GUN DECK

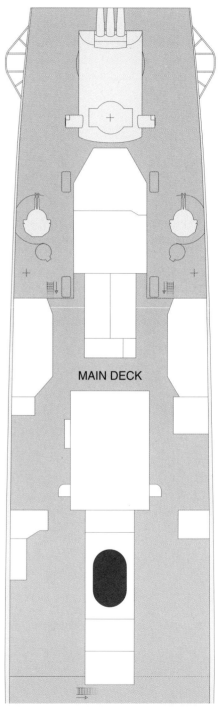

MAIN DECK

December 17, 1943 - The "Louie's" aircraft crane is swung out to starboard, perhaps to catch a "Seagull".

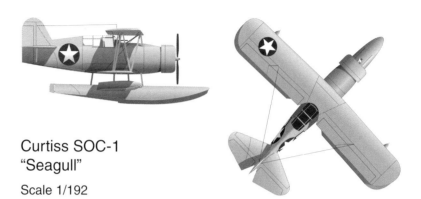

Curtiss SOC-1 "Seagull"
Scale 1/192

35

A huge new main mast has been erected over the #2 funnel to accommodate forthcoming radar installations. The crew's shelter around the #2 funnel has been lowered and two of the 36 in. searchlights have been removed. Immediately aft, the existing structure has been enlarged to accept a second main battery director, a Mk 34. Further aft, a long "gallery" of 20 mm guns runs out to the newly installed Mk 33 DP gun director, still painted in the Measure 21. The ship in the next berth (left) is an old "four-stack" destroyer in the process of being converted to a APD.

36

A pair of 40 mm twin mountings on the stern have taken the place of troublesome 1.1 in quads. The little tubs adjacent are for the directors, Mk 51s. Another four 20 mm mounts surround the new Mk 33 which has retained the old Mk 4 radar screen of the previous director. Directly below, on the main deck, sits another 40 mm twin mount. One barrel has been removed, probably for servicing. Ditto on the port stern 40 mm.

8322-43
PLAN VIEW, AMIDSHIPS LOOKING AFT.
MARE ISLAND, CAL.   17 DECEMBER 1943.

(CA28).

8321-43   (CA28).
PLAN VIEW, AFT.
MARE ISLAND, CAL.   17 DECEMBER 1943.

February 6, 1945 - The next four photographs were probably taken as the Louisville entered port and show the kamikaze strikes of January 5, during the ship's operations in Lingayen Gulf, Philippines. The measure 32-6D is quite striking even though it is badly faded and in spots, burned! Compare with photo on page 31.

NO. 1 PLANE
CRASH

The oil and fuel lines running from the bow to the midship area were installed on the outside of the ship sometime in 1943. Should the lines be ruptured and ignited, the ensuing fire would not be inside the vessel.

NO. 1 PLANE
CRASH AREA

NO. 1 PLANE
CRASH

DIESEL OIL
LINE

GASOLINE
LINE

FRAGMENT HOLE
FROM NEAR MISS
BOMB. GASOLINE
& DIESEL OIL LINES
RUPTURED.

The first Kamikaze hit was largely ricocheted overboard. The second hit was directly into the side of the superstructure on the starboard. Temporary repairs were carried out by the crew as soon as possible. A crude pipe rail has been erected on the signal bridge to replace the damaged shielding which had to be cut away. Part of the shielding and flooring on the navigation level has been shredded.

NO 2 PLANE CRASH AREA

GASOLINE FIRE DAMAGE

NO 1 PLANE CRASH

TURRET No. 2

④

893-45   CA 28
NO. 1 AND 2 PLANE CRASHES
STARBOARD SIDE CLOSE-UP VIEW
MARE ISLAND, CALIF   6 FEB. 1945

Port-side damage was very minimal. On the main deck, foreward of the catapult silo, 8in. shells and powder charges are stacked, ready to be off-loaded. Prior to the beginning of repairs to the ship, all munitions and fuels will be removed to avoid accidental ignition.

NO. 1 PLANE CRASH

GASOLINE FIRE DAMAGE FROM NO. 2 PLANE CRASH

2

STBD. SIDE OF
VENTURI WINDSHIELD
CRUSHED BY NO.1
PLANE

TURRET NO. 2
DAMAGED BY
BOMB EXPLOSION

60# S.T.S.
PL.

NO.1 PLANE CRASH

COMMUNICATION
PLATFORM

SPRAY SHIELD DISTORTED

5

920-45
NO.1 PLANE CRASH
AND BOMB DAMAGE - LOOKING AFT AT
8" GUN TURRET NO. 2
MARE ISLAND, CALIF.   7 FEB. 1945

CA 28

February 7, 1945; Mare Island - Three dramatic photographs taken on board detail damage inflicted by the two Japanese suicide crashes. At left, the results of the first kamikaze which hit on the top of #2 turret, careened into the front of the navigation bridge and toppled into the sea off the starboard side. Fortunately for the Louisville, the crashing plane hit one of the best protected parts of the ship and caused much less damage than it could have. Suicide pilots would attempt to crash an enemy ship in the area of the bridge to disrupt navigation and kill as many officers as possible. The attacking plan called for the pilot to release a small bomb (if possible) just prior to impact, hopefully causing two explosions.

41

Close-up photos show the heavier damage caused by the second kamikaze strike in the starboard side superstructure. (left) Most of the casualties occured in this lightly protected area. The plane crash took out the quad 40mm anti-aircraft gun on the command level and the adjacent single 20mm mount. Fire from the aircraft's ruptured fuel tanks engulfed the immediate area. (right) The suicide plane's motor broke free slamming a massive dent in the #1 funnel and spreading the fire. Notice the scorched paint on the front of the funnel.

DESTROYED
20 MM. GUN
REPLACED

NAV.
BR.

DECK CUT AWAY?

STBD. BOMB
EXPLOSION
DAMAGE

SIGNAL BRIDGE

PATH OF NO 2 PLANE

COMM
FL

STBD. 40MM.
QUAD. NO.1 DESTROYED
BY PORT BOMB
EXPLOSION FROM
NO.2 PLANE CRASH

(15)

926-45   CA 28
NO. 2 PLANE CRASH
& BOMB DAMAGE - LKG. DOWN, AT FR. 50, ON
STBD. SIDE FROM TOP OF CHART HOUSE
MARE ISLAND, CALIF.   7 FEB. 1945

NO.1 STACK & AFT. BULWARK
BUCKLED BY WRECKAGE &
IMPACT OF NO. 2 PLANES
MOTOR.

4'

2'   NO.1
STACK

FR. 56

SIGNAL BR.

(14)

28-45   CA 28
NO. 2 PLANE CRASH
AMAGE AT AFT. END OF SIGNAL BRIDGE &
TACK NO.1 - LOOKING TO STARBOARD.

41

March 25, 1945: Mare Island - Nearing completion of the repairs and refitting, Louisville is receiving new paint in the form of Measure 22: overall Haze Gray (5-H) with a wide "false waterline" in Navy Blue (5-N) above the boot topping. On the bow, a 40mm position is under construction. A Mk28 fire control radar has been fitted to the Mk33 DP director forward of the charthouse. Two observation blisters have been added to the shield around the navigation deck.

20mm gun positions have been removed from the sides of the #1 funnel. On this side, three life rafts will be stored on the side of the funnel enclosure. On the starboard side, an extra pontoon will be stowed for the three Curtiss SC-1 Seahawks she now carries. The starboard catapult and tower have been landed.

2181-45
(CA28)
PLAN VIEW, AMIDSHIPS LOOKING AFT.
INCLINING EXPERIMENT

A new 20mm gun position has been constructed on the side of the enclosure around #2 funnel. Sitting between two unfinished ammunition lockers is a 20mm mount in the newer twin configuration on a lighter Mk10 pedestal. Some 20mm gun positions were eliminated; the remaining single mounts were replaced by the newer twin version.

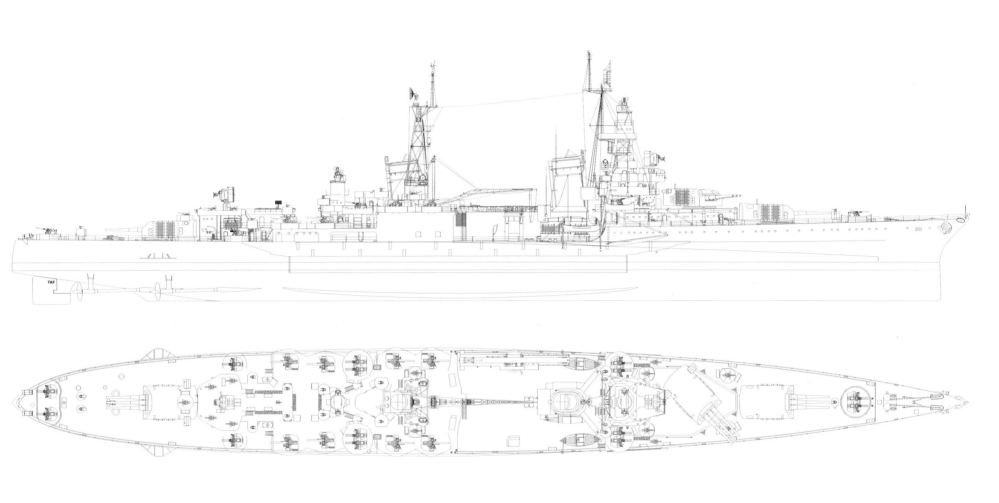

USS Louisville
April, 1945

scale 1/700

2536-45 (CA28)
PLAN VIEW, FORWARD.
MARE ISLAND, CAL. 10 APRIL 1945.

2539-45
PLAN VIEW AMIDSHIPS AND FORW.
MARE ISLAND, CAL. 10 APRIL 1945

April 10, 1945: Mare Island - The USS Louisville readies for departure back to the Pacific war. (left) White circles highlight new paravane handling gear on the bow and a new quad 40mm position in front of #1 turret. Behind #2 turret on the navigation level is a new wind screen complete with canvas canopy. (above) A huge new machinery space vent (lower center) replaces the starboard catapult and tower. Also the number of seaplanes was reduced to iliminate top weight. Other circled items: the new 20mm position abreast the #2 funnel, a section of the crane was strengthened and a spare float plane pontoon strapped on the starboard side of the #1 funnel.

April 10, 1945 - (above) The mainmast erected in '43 now supports a massive array of ECM (Electric Countermeasures) antennas. At the top of the mast extension is the TDY jammer. Its two dipoles, mounted back to back, allow for the coverage of two frequency ranges. The two small circular antenna on the ends of the arm are TBS tactical radio. (right) A SP fighter control radar unit has been installed on the back of the radar platform. Its rotating 8 ft. screen could detect both airborne and surface targets. Depending on the object, range extended out to 70 nm. On the Mk 34 main director, a Mk 13 replaces the older Mk 8 battery fire control.

(left) In the center of the photo, circled, sits a small portable SQ emergency search radar unit; maximum range was 8nm. Other circled items include the installation of additional Mk51 units. Some of these units were installed in the tubs vacated by single 20mm guns. (above) The midship quad 40mm gun has received a Mk34 fire control antenna mounted on its left. The square structure below the gun's tub is a collection bin for the spent 40mm shells. A domed S-band TDY jammer sits just forward and a similar unit has been fitted halfway up the tripod mainmast.

Another look at the new Mk 13 radar. The actual screen was an 8 ft x 2 ft parabola which rocked up and down within the radome shell. A close look at the inside of the 40 mm shielding reveals a multitude of little boxes. While the ship is on duty, these boxes are filled with 4-round clips for the 40 mm guns, ready for immediate use. The secondary fire director has received a new radar dish; a Mk 28.

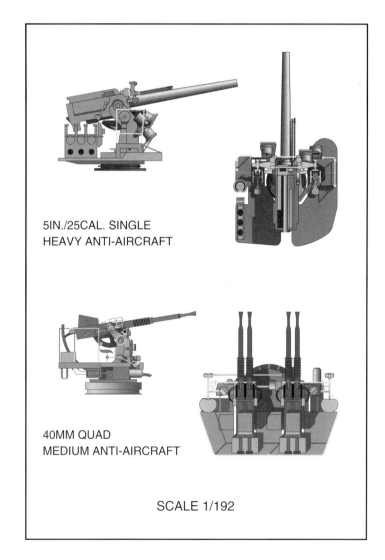

5IN./25CAL. SINGLE
HEAVY ANTI-AIRCRAFT

40MM QUAD
MEDIUM ANTI-AIRCRAFT

SCALE 1/192

USS LOUISVILLE

APRIL, 1945

SCALE 1/350

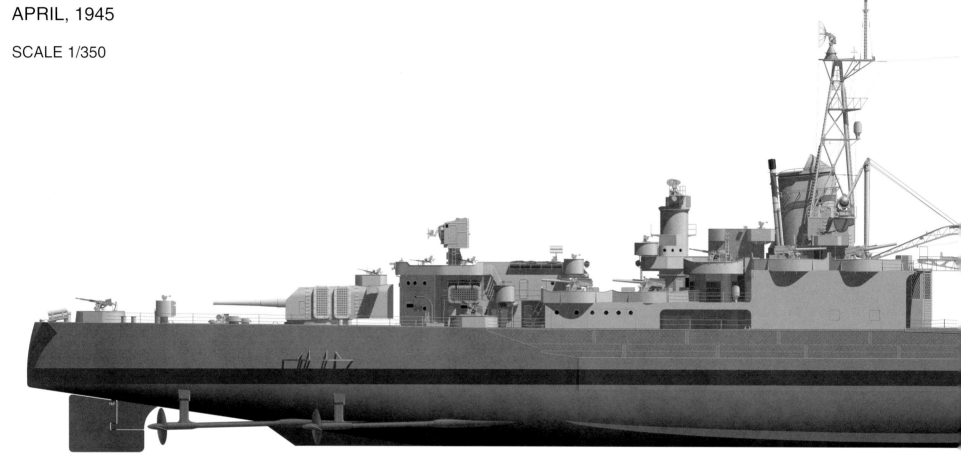

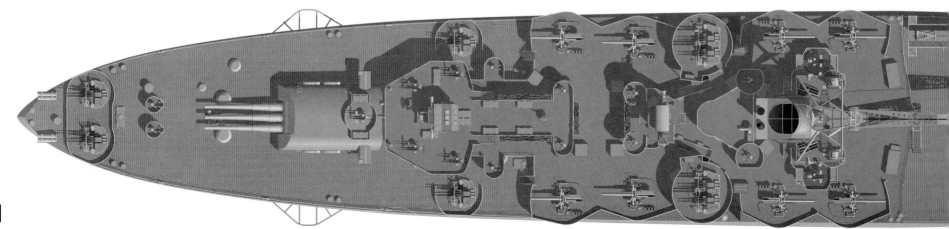

MEASURE 22 CAMOUFLAGE

Vertical Surfaces
Haze Gray (5-H)
Navy Blue (5-N)

Horizontal Surfaces
Weatherdeck Blue (20-B)

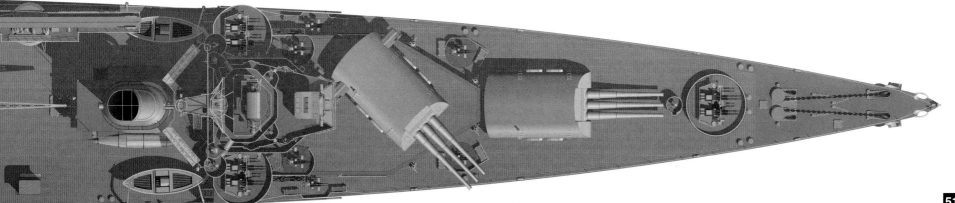

April 10, 1945 - Her refit complete, the Louisville soon sails for the Pacific to team up with Task Force 58 and the assault on Okinawa. A new quad 40mm mount on the bow should help discourage the next kamikaze pilot from coming in for a low end-on attack.

America's war material production was supplying the latest technology and in vast quantities. The Louisville leaves with the latest radar upgrades and an awesome anti-aircraft arsenal.

Seagulls abound when a ship enters or leaves port because the fishing always gets better. The ship's turbulence stuns or kills small fish near the surface and the gulls find the pickin's easy.

June 6, 1945 - Despite her massive air defense force, the USS Louisville was hit again by a determined Japanese pilot. The #1 funnel collapsed from the impact but this time the fires were minimal and the suicide plane again careened over the starboard side. Fifty-nine men were injured but only one fatally. The crash occurred while she was on station off Okinawa on the evening of the 5th.

After her sale to the Marlene Blouse Corporation of New York, Louisville is readied for her last journey. Most of the small equipment (radar, antennas, 20mm guns, etc) have been removed previously. She is painted Haze Gray (5-H) with eight foot hull numbers. She will be scrapped in November, 1959. A sad end to a gallant veteran.

GENERAL STATISTICS

Authorized
1927

Builder
Puget Sound Navy Yard
Bremerton, Washington

Keel Laid
July 4, 1928

Launched
September 1, 1930

Commissioned
January 15, 1931

Dimensions
length overall ....600.00 ft.
length waterline ....582.00 ft.
beam ....66.00 ft.
draught   (min.)............16.25 ft.
              (max.)...........23.50 ft.

Displacement
light ....9,277 tons
standard ....10,965 tons
full load - 1931 ....11,826 tons
              1944 ....14,030 tons

Armor
main belt ....3 to 3.75 in.
decks.....................1 to 2 in.
turrets ....1.5 to 2.5 in.
magazines..................1.5 in.
conning tower.............1.5 in.

Aircraft
1930 - 1936..........Vought O3U Corsair (4)
1936 - 1945 ....Curtiss SOC Seagull (4)
1945.................Curtiss SC-1 Seahawk (3)

Compliment
1931 ....45 officers, 576 enlisted men
1945 ....68 officers, 1061 enlisted men

Propulsion
Boilers ....White-Forster water tube type
Engines ....4 Parsons geared turbines
Speed ....32.75 kts. at 109,000 shp

Fuel
standard...................1417 tons
full load - 1931 ....2125 tons
                1945 ....2957 tons

Endurance
1931 ....10,000 nm. at 15 kts.
1945 ......7,285 nm. at 15 kts.
              5,250 nm. at 20 kts.

Decommissioned
June 17, 1946

Cost to build
$9 million (1931)

ARMAMENT SUMMARY		1931	1934	1940	1942	1943	1944	1945
main battery	8 in./55 cal	9	9	9	9	9	9	9
heavy anti-aircraft	5 in./25 cal	4	4	8	8	8	8	8
	3 in./50 cal	–	–	4	4 to 0	–	–	–
light anti-aircraft	40 mm	–	–	–	–	0 to 24	24	24 to 28
	20 mm	–	–	–	0 to 19	19 to 27	27	27 to 26
	1.1 in	–	–	–	0 to 16	16 to 0	–	–
	.50 cal	8	8	12	12 to 0	–	–	–
torpedo tubes	21 in	6	–	–	–	–	–	–

REFERENCES

American Cruisers of WWII: S. Ewing
Cruisers of WWII: M.J. Whitley
Fighting Ships: Maclean & Poole
U.S.Cruisers: N. Friedman
U.S. Naval Weapons: N. Friedman

RESOURCES

United States Navy
U.S. Naval Historical Center
Tom Walkowiak's Floating Drydock
Real War Photos
Cosiar Armada Products

CLASSIC WARSHIPS PUBLISHING

extends a very special thanks to

Don Montgomery
Robert Sumeral
Mike Davis
Tom Sherwood
and the staff at CBC

Listed below are some of our favorite sources for reference books, photographs, plans and models

REAL WAR PHOTOS
P.O.Box 728
Hammond, Indiana 46325
catalog $3

PACIFIC FRONT HOBBIES
11804 NE 138th Street
Kirkland, Washington 98034
Ph. 206-821-2564

THE FLOATING DRYDOCK
c. o. general delivery
Kresgeville, Pennsylvania 18333
catalog $10

U. S. NAVAL INSTITUTE
2062 Generals Hwy.
Annapolis, Maryland 21401
Ph. 800-233-8764

TAUBMAN PLANS SERVICE
11 College Drive #4
Jersey City, New Jersey 07305
catalog $10